1 + 2 = 3

1 + 2 = 3

A Proven Step-by-Step Guide to Solving Staffing and Coworker-Turnover Issues in any Business

By Christopher T. Henderson

© 2019 by Christopher T. Henderson

All rights reserved. This book or any portion thereof may not be reproduced or used in any manner whatsoever without the express written permission of the publisher except for the use of brief quotations in a book review.

ISBN: 9781699205310

Preface

I was a general manager (GM) of a national brand restaurant company when I received a phone call from our corporate office. The caller identified himself as Mark upon introduction. Mark was a graduate student at the University of Tennessee and was working on his thesis while also working in the human resources department of our corporate office. After his introduction, Mark stated he was reaching out to the general managers throughout our company, who achieved the lowest coworker-turnover results, in order to learn why coworkers would leave their positions in the restaurant industry.

I remember thinking, "What a strange question," and then responded to Mark by saying, "Well, Mark, they actually tell you their reason for leaving right on the application." The most common response I remember was poor management. I said, "Think about it. Most coworkers leaving are not leaving the restaurant industry. They are going from Applebee's to TGI Fridays to Chili's, et cetera. The industry is good. They like the schedule flexibility; they like the coworkers (friends) they work with, the cash tips, the overtime, et cetera. What they are looking for are new managers." I stated to Mark, "Coworkers are not looking for new jobs. They are looking for new managers." The job is good in their eyes.

Now, when I say "looking for new managers," does this mean that those managers with high-coworker turnover do not care about their business or their people? Absolutely not! This simply speaks to the poor leadership skills, disorganization, poor communication, and lack of a disciplined approach by the management team, all of which lead to a frustrating work environment. The coworkers who are leaving one restaurant company for another are looking for leaders who run great operations. Additionally, the general manager sets the tone for that environment.

This book is focused entirely on step one of the 1 + 2 = 3 philosophy, with the first step being the focus of systems in place for filling your operation with great coworkers. You see, 1 + 2 = 3 refers to the following: coworkers (1), guests (2), and owners/shareholders (3). It seems simple and, to a degree, it is. However it is not bad luck, or just the way the industry is, that causes this revolving door of coworkers leaving one restaurant company for another. Decades of lessons learned and the development of systems, which address issues that frustrate coworkers, are explained throughout this book. 1 + 2 = 3 is a step-by-step approach of how a *great-place-to-work* environment is created in order to grow teams, guests, and ultimately profitability. This is achieved only through a dedicated focused plan of systems, which are proven to lower coworker turnover to a healthy level.

First, I want establish a truth: by no means should your coworker-turnover goal be set at zero turnover. Not only is this simply unrealistic, but more importantly, a zero-coworker-turnover goal would be unhealthy for your business. People are going to relocate, grow tired of the grind associated with the hospitality industry, finish their education, or move on to another career path. The goal of lowering coworker turnover should be to achieve the lowest level possible for all of the right reasons; in other words, to never hold on to a coworker who is impacting your business negatively for the sake of a lower turnover percentage. It is critical to understand that when we hold on to problem coworkers for too long and for the sake of achieving a better number on paper, ultimately we are delaying our goal of achieving a great-place-to-work environment.

It is very common to see general managers and their management teams want to bypass the work of step one, consisting of coworkers (creating a great-place-to-work environment) and simply build sales and profit. Although there are many examples of operations with same-store sales increases and improved profits, even with their high-coworker turnover, those results often are not sustained for long periods of time. In order to build step two (guests) of the 1 + 2 = 3 philosophy, you must surround yourself with the right people who understand their job responsibilities at a very high level. The competitive environment of the restaurant industry in particular demands that. High-coworker turnover halts the personal development that is necessary for coworkers to execute their job responsibilities at the highest level required for sales and profitability growth. It is impossible to consistently execute on a high level for the guests when you are constantly filling the open spots of coworkers who are leaving for another management team. This sounds simple but only through a deliberate plan and a change in behaviors will coworker turnover be lowered to the healthy levels we are seeking. It is actually anything but easy; however, it *can* be done! Again I stress the goal is healthy turnover results not a goal of zero-coworker turnover.

As mentioned above, many general managers want to jump directly to step three (owners/shareholders) of the 1 + 2 = 3 philosophy by increasing profit and putting money in the bank. That is a natural desire due to the fact that profit is the reason behind the business. However, many operators try to squeeze profit by cutting costs instead of driving top-line sales increases (step two, guests). In addition, many operators want to drive top-line sales increases (step two, guests) before putting in the focused, hard work of developing a team that can execute on a consistently high level. Why do sports dynasty, championship teams continuously challenge for championships? It's because of their teams' ability to consistently execute on a higher level than their competition. If you want championship results, you must first build a championship team.

This book will share many practices, philosophies, and systems for driving coworker turnover to industry-leading, low levels. Again, this is not easy work to do, and luck will have nothing to do with the results. However, the results will be the product of a clear and focused plan, with the end result being healthy coworker-turnover levels that provide a great-place-to-work environment.

Contents

1. Understanding Coworker Turnover 1
2. Know Where You Have Been, in Order to Know Where You Are Going 5
3. Hire Nice People—Not People You Have to Tell to Be Nice 13
4. A Look Back at History: The Misconception of Reference Checks 19
5. Crossing the Bridge—Getting Started with a New Company 23
6. Training—The Pal Barger Way 27
7. My Perfect Schedule 29
8. Creating a Fair and Disciplined Environment 33
9. Coaching—Don't Just Walk on By 39
10. Internal Communication 43
11. Developing Your Managers for the Future 47
12. Leadership: What Exactly Does That Look Like? 53
13. Closing: The Law of Business 59

Author Biography 63

Chapter 1:

Understanding Coworker Turnover

Denial is the worst enemy of personal growth. Blame and excuses follow closely behind. To truly achieve the healthy coworker-turnover results that we desire and need to compete effectively in this era of oversaturated markets, we must take an honest look at our current leadership skills and accept that *we* are the catalyst for the frustrating work environment. However, this may be a tough pill to swallow. Until you accept that your leadership skills can grow and that you actually *own* the results of coworker turnover, you are likely to continue the same practices and achieve the same results.

When we live in denial, we often have our blinders on, in regard to the opportunities that would help us grow our business and achieve an improved quality of life. That improved quality of life is often found in the reduction of stress by surrounding ourselves with the right people. Even if improved operations, sales, and profits do not entirely motivate you, surely, understanding the positive impact of an improved quality of life for you and your team will motivate you to apply these systems. To reduce our levels of denial, I encourage you to thoroughly consider the following three principles, accept them as the *three truths* that they are, and strive to change your outlook regarding coworker turnover.

Truth one is that coworker turnover is a *choice*. Coworker turnover is a result of behaviors and decisions we make as leaders. It has nothing to do with good or bad luck; it is all about the choices we make on a daily basis as the leaders of our business. Examples of some of those poor choices are as follows: poor selection decisions, poor interviewing techniques, poor communication between management and the coworkers, poor scheduling, lack of fair accountability of our people, favoritism, and poor training—and the list goes on and on. Fortunately, once you recognize these behaviors and the negative impact they have on your business, these choices can be corrected. Few things positively impact coworker turnover quicker than understanding the behaviors we choose that drive the results we are experiencing. Not only are we able to learn how our choices impact our business, but we also control those negative behaviors as individuals.

Truth two is that coworker turnover is a *money* skill, not a *soft* skill. The Center for Hospitality Research at Cornell University estimates that the cost of coworker turnover averages approximately $5,864 per person for a typical front-line coworker, which is broken down as follows: predeparture, $176; recruiting, $1,173; selection, $645; orientation and training, $821; and productivity loss (P&L), $3,049 (gradual expense over time).

The productivity-loss impact is sometimes the most difficult for us to comprehend, because it is a very long, drawn-out result and not the immediate negative impact on your P&L, as a case of sirloins walking out the back door would impact your food cost immediately. That lack of productivity is very sneaky and very difficult to see. I encourage you to think back to an opening shift on a Sunday morning, when you notice your lineup of opening cooks are all very new in position and very underdeveloped in their training. Your stomach sinks a bit, because you know what lies ahead. Now compare that feeling to an opening shift on a Sunday morning with your lineup of opening cooks who are all veterans and have a very high skill level. You experience a completely different quality of life in that moment. The difference in skill level and productivity is the driving force behind the lack of stress in that moment.

In regards to the sneaky cost of productivity, even taking a very conservative approach, it is conceivable that each coworker turned over in the restaurant business costs nearly $2,000 each. If you are losing five to eight coworkers or more each month, that loss of profit increases quickly, while the negative impact of the weaker execution on top-line sales drives profitability in a negative direction.

I have had many one-on-one conversations over the years discussing this very point about coworker turnover actually being a *money* skill rather than a *soft* skill.

It might just be possible that, in all of those conversations, I experienced a reaction from the person I was talking with. That reaction is what I call the *nod* conversation. What I have found is that almost everyone agrees with the negative impact that high-coworker turnover has on their P&L; therefore, they nod in agreement. However, if the *nod* is the only result from the conversation, then behaviors do not change and neither do the results. There is a direct correlation between the leadership abilities of management and the coworker-turnover result.

Truth three is that coworker turnover is not driven by the *market*. Rather than accepting the fact that our behaviors drive the negative performance with coworker turnover, many operators justify the revolving door of coworkers by blaming it on the market. It is common to hear operators say, "We just can't find good people in this area." The truth is you can put a great leader into any market, give them time, and they will surround themselves with great coworkers while reducing turnover results. Now, I admit, some markets are tougher than others. Therefore, it is realistic to say it may take longer in certain markets. However, those fifty to one hundred coworkers your operation needs are there. You just have to have time to build the team. If the wrong mindset is present with that operational leadership team, then the behaviors will not change, and the excuses will continue. When the right beliefs and systems are in place, the results are positive in *any* market.

In order to really move forward in this journey of lowering coworker turnover to a healthy level, you must fully accept these three philosophies as truth and eliminate the denial. Coworker turnover is a choice, and that choice is absolutely a *money skill*. The market does not determine your coworker-turnover results.

Chapter 2:

Know Where You Have Been, in Order to Know Where You Are Going

There is an old saying when dealing with any problem: "First and foremost, you must stop the bleeding." In order to stop the bleeding, you must know where and why the bleeding exists in the first place. This is an example of denial coming into play. If we continue to do what we have been doing, why would we assume our results are going to improve as we move forward? If you want a different result, it is going to take a change in your mindset regarding your behaviors. I assume it is simply human nature for us to be in denial and that we are actually the problem. After all, we are working as hard as we can. So how can anyone expect more from us? The issue has nothing to do with how hard a leader is working. It has everything to do with their choices and behaviors.

Jack Nicholson is regarded as one of Hollywood's best. One of his most famous lines comes from a scene with Tom Cruise in the film *A Few Good Men*. Cruise is pressuring Nicholson in a courtroom setting, and Nicholson responds with one of the greatest lines of all time, "You can't handle the truth!" My question to you as a leader: Can you handle the truth? The only way we grow in our development is when we are fortunate enough to have someone who is honest with us. If you work with a boss who has the courage to tell you the truth about your performance, consider yourself fortunate! You have the opportunity to change your behavior and grow, due to the fact you have someone who cares enough about you.

Often it is more difficult for coworkers to talk openly and honestly due to fear. In order to position yourself for that truth, you have to genuinely develop trust. Trust is the result of your behaviors and reactions when dealing with coworkers on a daily basis. It cannot be *faked* once you decide to seek their feedback. The development of trust is built over a long period of time with consistent, professional behaviors and reactions, especially when things become stressful. It is easy to be a leader when everything is going well, but what are your behaviors when things are a bit chaotic? That is when you are truly building trust.

This leads us to the first *choice* of behaviors in our new quest of achieving a great-place-to-work environment. The choice of asking, listening, and then learning for the sake of getting better. There are basically two systems of feedback where we can hope to gain valuable information from the coworkers we work with: coworker stay interviews and coworker exit interviews. Coworker stay interviews result in feedback from our team who currently work with us. This is where the trust we develop with our people on a daily basis benefits us. The following are three simple questions I have asked when sitting down with coworkers for a stay interview.

Question one: "What are your goals outside of work?" It is critical that this is the first question. Until you prove to your team that you respect them as the real people they are, with real lives outside of the workplace and with real goals and aspirations (even on really good days and really bad days), then they are unlikely to be interested in helping you achieve your goals. If you do not know what is important to them outside of work, then you really do not know what their driving force is. For some of your coworkers, their driving force might be to graduate from college; for others, being the best mom possible while working to help support the family. All of us have those things that drive us. Knowing the priorities of your team creates a sense of security and respect for the coworkers as the real people they are.

Question two: "What are your goals while working with us?" For some, the answer may be, "I need to earn three hundred dollars each week in order to pay my bills." Or you might hear, "I need to make enough money to pay for my basics while I finish school." Someone else might say, "I love this company, and this is what I want to do as my career. I want to become a manager and then become a GM someday."

Question three: "If you had a magic wand and could change *anything* about this workplace, but only one thing, what would that one thing be?" This is the test of whether or not *you* can handle the truth. Great leaders don't stay wrong for long.

Great leaders look for how they can improve as well as constantly grow their business. When we reach that point where we feel we have our business figured out and we do not need to make changes, we have reached the point where we begin to decline. There is an old saying, "The only way to coast is on the way down." Think about it—you cannot coast while going up!

Every company boasts they have an open door policy. What exactly does that mean? How does an open door policy work? It really comes back to that word trust. Please remember, trust is built every day through the consistent behaviors and reactions you show. Do you take your people for granted, or do you really appreciate the fact they are there and ready to help you grow your business? A system for developing a true open door policy is by choosing one hour each week that you as the general manager reserve for one-on-one conversations with your people. This has to be a long-term system that allows you to build credibility and trust with them as the real people they are.

Let's say, for example, you and your company perform weekly inventories on Wednesday evenings. More than likely, you schedule yourself each and every Wednesday in order to complete this task. The one hour that you reserve for one-on-one conversations is an investment you are making into growing your business. Initially, your coworkers are not going to understand the point of these one-on-one meetings. You should prepare to *recruit* some people to go first in order to help you grow this system. The one hour should be time on your schedule blocked off into four fifteen-minute, one-on-one meetings utilizing a sign-up sheet as shown below.

Matt's Commitment to a True Open-Door Policy

Each week I will post a sign-up sheet for a scheduled one-on-one meeting with me to discuss your goals, possible improvements to the restaurant, or anything else you would like to discuss.

First come, first served.
Wednesday 9/4/2019

4:00–4:15 p.m.	_____
4:15–4:30 p.m.	_____
4:30–4:45 p.m.	_____
4:45–5:00 p.m.	_____

If your schedule does not work with this time frame, come see me, and we can schedule a time that will work for both of us!
Thank you!
Matt, GM, Store 123

- The following are several important things to remember regarding these open-door, one-on-one meetings (stay interviews):
- Always sit down at these one-on-one meetings with something to write with to take notes. When people see we are taking notes, we are showing their thoughts are important to us.
- Utilize the three questions outlined above in order to generate the conversation, but allow them to do the talking. Ask follow-up questions in order to go deeper into the subject, but allow them to express their thoughts.
- Don't be defensive when you hear feedback that might actually be helpful in growing your business. These conversations are designed to help you grow your business. Their perspective is their reality, even if it doesn't emulate your perspective. You will not develop trust by turning your open door policy into a debate. Just because you write it down, doesn't mean you will not have a different perspective. Keep the conversation positive.
- Make it a productive conversation, and ask the coworker to encourage their peers to sign up for an open door, one-on-one meeting.

The second type of feedback we can gain from coworkers is called an exit interview. These are not always easy to achieve, nor are they always easy to digest. However, it is critically important to try to reconnect with coworkers who have left you for other managers in order to understand *why*. It is typically best to allow some time after the coworker leaves in order to attempt to gain the exit interview participation. An example of a typical exit interview questionnaire is shown below.

Exit Interview Questions

Coworker name:

Date:

Manager conducting exit interview:

1. What made you feel as if you needed to begin looking for a new job?
2. What ultimately led you to accept the new position?
3. Do you feel you had the tools to do your job?
4. How would you describe the culture of our company
5. What could have been done in order for you to remain employed here?
6. Did you share your concerns with anyone at the company?
7. If you could change anything about your job or the company, what would you change?
8. Management is often a key factor in a coworker's decision to leave. Were you satisfied with the way you were managed?
9. Did you receive feedback regarding how you were performing your job?
10. Would you consider returning to our company and if so, what would need to change in your eyes?

At this point, we now have two systems for obtaining valuable information for improving your business from your people: open door one-on-ones with your current team and exit interviews with coworkers who are no longer on your team. In order to *know where you have been to know where you are going,* keeping a record of why people are leaving is critical. Coworker-turnover logs are the history books that will point you in the right direction. You see, coworker turnover is usually the result of one of three areas: poor selection (interviewing), poor onboarding/training, and poor environment.

By keeping a log of coworkers who leave for another management team, you will be able to see where you have been in order to know where you need to go. In other words, it will be clear which behaviors need to be adjusted to reach your desired outcome. To really understand why coworkers are leaving you in search of new managers, it is valuable to analyze the individual situations of each and every coworker who has left. An example of a simple coworker-turnover log is shown below.

Period/Year	Great-Place-to-Work Turnover Log			Restaurant: (enter below)
1/2019				#2222 Hollywood, Florida
Instructions: reason for termination 1. Selection 2. Orientation/Training 3. Environment 4. Relocation				
Coworker Name	Hire Date	Termination Date	Position	Reason for Termination
Charlie Example	1/3/2019	1/27/2019	Utility	Selection: NC/NS
Betty Leftus	12/4/2018	1/28/2019	Server	Training: did not train Betty with only certified trainers. She was trained by one of our newest servers, and there were several things we missed in her training
Ken Nomore	1/20/19	1/27/19	Dish	Selection: NC/NS
Johnny Wentaway	12/12/18	2/1/19	Cook	Selection: NC/NS

Having the courage to be honest with yourself in regards to why you are losing coworkers to other management teams is a great strength. Rarely do we learn from our successes. However, when we have the courage to take on the truths of our opportunities, real growth occurs. The coworker-turnover log is a waste of effort if you do not have the courage to be 100 percent honest, even when we make mistakes. There is no shortcut or easy path to lowering coworker turnover; however, the payoff is huge when we arrive. Not only does the execution of our operation drastically improve, but quality of life for management improves as well. Remember the scenario described during that opening shift on Sunday morning? You are looking around at the talent (or lack of) you are working with—quality of life for management!

By knowing where you have been, you are able to make operational changes to your approach in improving your quality of life. As you continue to read this book, you will continue to be exposed to proven systems that aid in creating a great-place-to-work environment. Once coworkers feel you are successful in creating a great-place-to-work environment, then they no longer feel the need to find new managers.

Chapter 3:

Hire Nice People—Not People You Have to Tell to Be Nice

During the interview and selection process, I see many managers who are overly concerned with the applicant's previous experience level. I challenge you to think differently. Rather than focusing on the applicant's previous experience level, ask yourself a question: Are we able to teach this person the tasks of what we need them to do? Then ask yourself a second question: Are we able to teach this person the manners, kindness, generosity, friendliness, ability to communicate, unselfishness, teamwork mentality, and overall ability to serve others?

As you consider your answers to those questions, I encourage you to have less value for the experience level they are bringing, because you can train them to do the things you need for your business. However, you cannot teach grown adults how to act. As adults, we are wired the way the way we are, and ultimately you are not going to change that wiring. By no means am I saying people cannot learn and grow. We are able to learn new tasks and perspectives. However, a person's natural disposition is often going to determine *fit* in the hospitality business.

While a student at Virginia Tech, I had the ability to decide what major I wanted to focus on. In reading about Virginia Tech's Hospitality and Tourism Management program, the very first statement in the description of the program stated, "You must truly enjoying working with all different types of people." How true that statement is. The fact of the matter is not everyone enjoys working with all different types of people. For some, it comes natural; for others it simply does not. For some, smiling and being gracious in other people's wants and desires comes naturally; for others it simply does not exist. In other words, not everyone is cut out for the hospitality industry, and that is okay. However, trying to fit the square peg into the round hole has rarely worked.

Now, I will focus on the more *technical* part of the selection/hiring process: interviewing. Throughout my career, I have sat in on countless interviews with less-experienced managers conducting the interview in order to observe their interview skills. Nearly 100 percent of the time that I observe interviews, the manager asks the questions by relying on their memory. From my observations, when a manager is relying on their memory to think of the next question to ask, they generally are thinking to themselves, "What question am I going to ask next?" Their mind is cluttered with trying to think of what's next. By allowing this *clutter* to occupy their thought process, they are no longer *listening* to the answers from the applicant. The result is a very poor interview, because we are not going below the surface with answers given by the applicant. In other words, the applicant responds with an answer that either simply does not make sense or simply is not true. Because of the clutter in our minds, we often miss these opportunities for follow-up questions such as, "Well, how exactly did that work?" or "Wow, that is very interesting. Can you tell me more about how that worked?" Instead, we quickly move on to the next question in an effort to appear *smooth* in the interview.

The solution to eliminating the clutter in our minds is with approaching 100 percent of our interviews with a list of structured interview questions. I have experienced managers being reluctant to taking a list of questions to the interview table, because they do not want to be viewed as a less-than-skilled manager, who must rely on a list of questions. Remember our discussion about denial and how coworker turnover is a result of our behaviors? Refusing to accept the advantages of utilizing a structured interview questions format is an example of those types of denial or behaviors.

Once we have a list of structured interview questions in front of us for the interview, we are now positioned to look at our notes, ask the applicant the question, and then listen to their response with intent and watch their body language. The whole point of conducting an interview is to try to assess who the person sitting across the table really is. Body language can tell you a different story than the words coming from their mouth. However, only you are zoned in, focused, and looking for the truth. When an applicant responds with an answer that simply doesn't make sense, stick with that subject and go deeper. Ask follow-up questions, such as: "How exactly did that work?" or "Can you tell me more about that?" When you ask a follow-up question, do they break eye contact and become fidgety or nervous, or do they respond with confidence and eagerness to tell you more about the situation?

In addition to helping you seek the truth with applicants, structured interview questions also help protect the business. By having the same format of questions with all applicants, there is no basis in the questions you are asking, which could be a form of discrimination. By asking everyone the same questions, you are providing an equal opportunity for all to potentially join your organization. It is important to take notes of the responses from the applicants and keep the structured interview questions with the applications. Not only does this provide protection for the organization but also truly provides a fair system for considering who you select in becoming a part of your team.

Below is a sample of structured interview questions. The first interviewer typically asks questions one through seven (the basics). If the first interviewer feels this applicant might actually be a good fit for our needs, then they move the applicant to the second interviewer. The second interviewer typically reviews the responses of questions one through seven and then proceeds with the remaining questions.

Structured Interview Questions

Applicant name _____

Date _____

Position applied _____

First Interview Questions

Motive

1. Are you currently working?
    - If yes: Are you looking to leave your current employer or work two jobs? What is your current pay rate?
    - If no: Where did you last work, and did you quit them or did they quit you? What was your hourly rate of pay?

2. What would be the perfect work schedule for you? Are there any days of the week or holidays you are unable to work?

	Thurs	Fri	Sat	Sun	Mon	Sat	Tue	Wed
a.m.								
p.m.								

Requested number of shifts each week you would like to be scheduled:

3. Do you have reliable transportation for getting to work?

Attitude
4. Tell me about your last job? What did you like best? What did you like least?

Dependability
5. What was your former manager's name? When I call _____, what is he/she goingto tell me about you?
6. What will your former manager tell me about your attendance?
7. What do you feel are acceptable reasons for calling out?

Second interview picks up here

Performance
8. What were some of the things you would do in your last job when it was slow?
9. In regard to your work history, what are you most proud of? Have you ever received any awards or been formally recognized for performance? If yes, tell me about it

Flexibility
10. Tell me about a time you helped someone and there was no benefit to yourself for helping them
11. Tell me about a time when the customer had a special request? How did you handle that?

Dependability
12. Tell me about a time you kept a promise you made to someone.

Hospitality
13. What things do customers do that you find annoying?
14. What does *hospitality* mean to you?

If you know this person is *not* qualified or a good fit for the open position, then explain the following:

We are interviewing a number of candidates for our open positions. If we feel you are one of the most qualified for the position,
either another manager or I will call you at _____
by tomorrow at 5:00 p.m.

If you do not hear from us by 5:00 p.m. tomorrow, then we have decided to move forward with someone we feel is more qualified. (Make certain to ask them again for the best number to reach them so they *know* that you know how to reach them.

Chapter 4:

A Look Back at History: The Misconception of Reference Checks

Once we have decided an applicant might just be a great fit and a solution to a staffing need, it is critical to contact previous employers listed on the application in order to get a reference check. Remember, the entire point of performing an interview is to assess exactly who this person is that is sitting in front of you and if they are the solution to your staffing need. History is often the best indicator of future performance. Not always, but it is often good to know if an applicant has walked out of their shift in the middle of a busy Sunday, or if they routinely run late for work.

Before you decide that no one will ever agree to provide the information you are seeking with your reference check, you should know that according to the American Bar Association Labor and Employment Law Section and Employment Rights and Responsibilities Committee (March 26, 2015), no state prohibits employers from giving out truthful information about a coworker's job performance. If the employer speaks in good faith, believing that the statements are true, then the employer isn't defaming the coworker. Providing the former coworker's rehire status is a very safe component to communicate to potential employers. Since courts view a manager's decision on the terminated coworker's rehire status as an *opinion*, courts support the manager's opinion of rehire status in litigation. Since that rehire status decision is a truthful and deliberate decision, decided upon by the management of the business, then there is no defamation in that decision to classify as *not rehirable*. That is the opinion of that management team.

Building relationships with other leaders within the five-mile ring of your operation is critical to the success of gaining reference checks. Reference checks have to be a two-way street. It is unreasonable to expect leaders of other businesses to provide truthful information to you in the form of a reference check if you refuse to provide the same courtesy. Trust is built upon truthful information. If you are not honest with the leaders contacting you regarding previous coworkers, the trust will not be built. On the other hand, if you provide truthful honest opinions regarding rehire status, then not only are you protecting your organization but also building relationships with other business leaders.

Defamation is a personal injury, which means a former employer could be held accountable for not only financial losses but also awarded damages for emotional distress. Defamation happens when someone makes an intentional false statement that harms another person. State rules differ on what a coworker must prove to win a defamation case. Generally speaking, the coworker must persuade the judge or jury of the following:

1. The employer made a false statement of fact about the coworker. A statement of opinion, for example, "I think Betty has a negative attitude," cannot be the basis of a defamation claim; nor can true statements, no matter how harmful.
2. The employer *published* the statement. In other words, the employer must actually make the statement to someone.
3. The employer knew or should have known the statement was false. If the employer believes, in good faith, that the statement is true, there is no defamation claim. However, if the employer acts with reckless disregard for the truth by representing a damaging and unsubstantiated rumor without checking into it, that might support a defamation claim.
4. The statement was not privileged. Many states recognize that candor and open communication are vital in certain relationships. Statements made in these contexts are privileged, which means that the speaker is protected from liability for making the statement. Many states protect the speaker as long as he or she acted without malice.

5. The coworker suffered harm because of the false statement. If the coworker has to prove damage, the harm usually involves another company's refusal to hire the coworker because of the false statement (NOLO, Defamation Lawsuits, Lisa Guerin).

Again, honesty is the basis for developing trust with other leaders within your five-mile ring. Your opinion is safe to share. However, make certain any statements made as a matter of fact are true, and you have no intent of harm, knowing your statement in unsubstantiated or false.

Chapter 5:

Crossing the Bridge—Getting Started with a New Company

The first day of working with a new company typically brings a mixture of excitement and apprehension. If you recall a time when you were the new person at the workplace, you more than likely experienced a mixture of emotions. However, the excitement may have been quickly replaced with fear and uncertainty. After all, there was so much to learn, and the people who were training you didn't always seem too happy to teach. Many times, the manager working on our first day didn't even know we were coming. Although this is not a great start, it is all too common in many industries.

You had looked forward to this day, but it seemed no one else did. You immediately start questioning whether this was the right place for you. As you looked around, everyone else seemed to have all of the answers. Everyone seemed as comfortable in their role as they could possibly be. You, on the other hand, didn't even know where the schedule was posted. Everyone else seemed to have been there forever and yet, you didn't even know where to stand without feeling like you were in somebody's way. This was not what you had imagined your first day was going to be like.

Initially, we felt like outsiders. That's because, in all reality, we were. We didn't feel as if we belonged, while everyone seemed to have fit in perfectly. There were cliques—you could see that immediately. There were some who worked together as a team and some who preferred to do everything alone. Your doubts and fears really started increasing. The question continued to pop into your head, "Did I make a mistake in wanting to work here?" Most people answer that question within the first thirty days of starting a new job.

Approximately ninety days seems to be a normal span of time in which coworkers reach the other side in *crossing the bridge*. The side where they feel comfortable and as if they belong. They feel they are part of the team. They no longer feel like they are outsiders. After approximately ninety days, coworker-turnover statistics drop dramatically. According to Fast Company spokesperson Stephanie Vozza and a survey conducted by Jobvite, coworkers who "voluntarily quit their jobs within the first ninety days, 43 percent say their day-to-day role wasn't what they expected, 34 percent report that an incident or bad experience drove them away, and 32 percent didn't like the company culture."

Just imagine, as a leader, if you had the ability to change that first day experience! What if there were things you could do as a leader that would aid the new coworkers in their transition to your operation? What if there were things you could do as a leader in order to help them in *crossing the bridge* and making it past the uncertainty of the first ninety days of working with your operation?

Remember the three truths in chapter one? Truth number one states coworker turnover is a choice. We are now presenting one of those choices (behaviors) that you make as a leader, which absolutely impacts how your new people feel on day one of employment with you. That choice is the decision you make as the general manager, regarding the importance of their orientation day. That choice is your role in their orientation. A great orientation for new coworkers is a system that must be in place. Not only should a great orientation be planned and executed, but as the general manager, it is a great investment of your time to spend quality time with the newly hired coworkers. As the general manager, you are often the most intimidating person with the operation. The quicker you can build trust as a leader, the easier it is for the new coworker to successfully cross the bridge. Sure, you can delegate the I-9s, tax forms, etc. section of the orientation to another manager. However, it is critical for the general manager to play a role in the new hire's orientation by taking the opportunity to allow the new coworkers to hear directly from their GM on the most important topics, which shape their work environment. Below is an example of some topics found on a general manager's orientation checklist.

1 + 2 = 3

GM Orientation Checklist

Date _____

Introductions: new coworkers, management team, trainers, staff, and regular guests.

Our goal is to be a great place to work

(great selection in the coworkers we chose, great training, writing of great schedules, great support).

Environment of respect: Respect as real people, not the roles we are playing.

Environment of accountability: Don't have to be a jerk, but I will hold you accountable through accurate and consistent note taking and discussions.

Call-out logs: One hundred percent of the callouts are recorded; two-hour minimum in order for us to be able to do our jobs as management of this business.

Tardy logs: Preshift meetings are scheduled five minutes after you are scheduled in. If you are late in joining us for the preshift meeting, then you are considered late for the shift.

The basic principle of any business: genuinely appreciate the fact our guests chose to spend their money in our restaurant.

We are really committed to being a great place to work. Therefore, I truly have an open-door policy. I will be scheduling some interviews with you over the next few weeks in order to see how you are doing.

Everyone experiences the awkward feeling of being new. I can't speed that process up for you; however, I promise it gets easier each time you return!

Chapter 6:

Training—The Pal Barger Way

Pal's Sudden Service is a twenty-six-unit restaurant company based out of Kingsport, Tennessee. Founded in the 1950s, Fred "Pal" Barger used his own *market research* (watching operations of other restaurant companies with his binoculars) in order to learn the business. Pal Barger went on to lead Pal's to become a well-oiled machine and even managed to win the *Malcom Baldridge National Quality* award, which is given by Congress and presented by the president of the United States. Other recipients of the award are Ritz-Carlton Hotel Company, Cadillac, and FedEx Corporation. Pal's Sudden Service is the first fast-food restaurant company to ever win the *Malcom Baldridge National Quality* award.

Why the unusual success for quality by a fast-food restaurant company? After all, it's just burgers, hot dogs, fries, and shakes. The simple answer is training. If you ever have the opportunity to experience the drive-thru at Pal's, you will understand. Oh, and by the way, there is no indoor seating or experience. Pal's Sudden Service operates on 100 percent drive-thru as their business model. As you pull up, you will notice the long line of cars wrapped around the building, down the street, and often blocking the entrance of their competitors. However, do not be intimidated by the long line of cars, because Pal's Sudden Service has mastered the art of getting cars through their drive-thru with an exceptionally high-speed and accuracy rate on orders.

As you reach the point of placing your order, you will not find a speaker box to speak into; you will be greeted by a well-trained coworker in the window. The coworker will take your order face-to-face, which is the beginning of the most pleasant fast-food experience you are likely to ever have. After ordering, you circle around the building to pay, where you will find a coworker who has been trained to anticipate and prepare for a cash payment by rounding up the change to the most likely payment, if there is a cash payment. If you pay with your card, it's not a problem. Either way, the anticipation of how you are likely to pay is part of the success with achieving the *sudden service*.

Pal's Sudden Service invests 120 hours of training for all new coworkers, and even then training never stops at Pal's. Every detail is important. Someone once asked Pal Barger about his investment in training by saying, "Pal, what if you invest all that money into training and the coworker leaves you?" Pal Barger responded, "What if I don't invest all that money into their training and they stay?"

Pal's Sudden Service currently operates twenty-six restaurant locations with an annualized coworker turnover rate of 32 percent. Management turnover is 1.4 percent annually, and Pal's has lost only seven general managers in thirty-three years. Pal's boasts that they are the "most profitable restaurant on the planet per square foot" of building space.

Thomas Crosby, chief executive officer (CEO) of Pal's Sudden Service, stated, "We realized that we are in the education business, just like any school or university. We want everyone we hire to be the equivalent of a valedictorian if we are going to beat the competition." Training includes everything from how to iron the Pal's uniform to statistical process control. Coworkers are certified for each skill position. Every shift, a computer selects names of two to four coworkers at each location to be recertified on a position skill. Each day the CEO and every other company's lead general managers and above spend 10 percent of their time helping a coworker develop a skill or aptitude. Crosby stated, "Every single day, everybody has to have a name and a subject they plan to work with them on. We ask, who are you working with today? It's just shorthand around here."

It is clear the investment into training continues to pay off for Pal's Sudden Service. Pal's leaders have become so skilled at training that they have opened their own leadership *university* in Kingsport, Tennessee, where operators from around the world bring their management teams to learn from the award-winning culture.

Chapter 7:

My Perfect Schedule

My wife and I have three college-age sons who have all worked in the restaurant business as servers and/or bussers. The restaurant where all three worked is a very nice steakhouse and one of our family's favorite places to dine. As normal, the cash tips were very good; however, the schedule writing was not. Many times our sons were scheduled for shifts they were unable to work due to other commitments such as school or athletic events. One of the easiest ways to keep your coworkers happy is to make a promise during their orientation regarding their schedules: I promise we will never schedule you when you have commitments outside of our workplace.

Why would any leader risk making such a promise? Because that leader is serious about creating a great-place-to-work environment. I advise you *not* to make that promise unless you are prepared to back it up. However, if you make that promise and keep it, you are making a significant impact on the personal lives of your coworkers. Feel confident during orientation to not only make that promise but to explain, "If we make a mistake and schedule you to work when you have communicated a commitment outside of work, we will cover the shift." The response you will hear is "Wow!"

Many companies work with computerized scheduling programs that allow you to block out times coworkers are unable to work. These scheduling programs make it even easier and more likely to avoid scheduling mistakes. The key to scheduling is communication through a system of coworkers completing an availability form, such as the one illustrated below. The premise is based on two scheduling factors: commitments and preferences. Commitments are those times where you are scheduled outside of work to another group of people or cause. Examples of these commitments are school, second jobs, child care, athletic teams, etc. Preferences are those times when coworkers don't have a commitment but they prefer to either work or not work based on many different reasons. For example, Mary might prefer to have Mondays off, because it is typically slow and she doesn't make much money.

Even though you can guarantee commitments, you cannot guarantee preferences. You should explain to the coworker that you will do your very best to honor the requested preference; however, you cannot guarantee both commitments and preferences. This promise has to also work both ways; meaning, when management needs to schedule a coworker during a time the coworker prefers off (yet has no commitment), the coworker must show the same respect for management by working the shift. If the coworker refuses to work the scheduled shift because they prefer off, it is no longer a two-way street, and the coworker is showing signs of a disengaged coworker. Place them on your *watch list* as someone who may become an upgrade situation in your effort of creating a great-place-to-work environment.

Once again, if a mistake is made with commitments, then management is responsible for covering that error, not the coworker. A not-so-great-place-to-work management team might say, "Well, I know you have school, and this error is our fault, but try to get someone to pick it up." That is *not* a great-place-to-work environment. This commitment to scheduling is a much higher level of leadership. Remember, coworkers are not leaving to find new jobs; they are leaving to find new managers—managers who can get their schedule right and not add stress to the coworker's life.

1 + 2 = 3

Commitment to Being a Great Place to Work Availability Form

Availability for _____

Date _____

Commitments: If you have a commitment outside of the restaurant such as second job, school, etc. we guarantee to not schedule you. Commitments must be communicated prior to schedules written on this form.

Preferences: If you prefer to work a specific shift, please write available in the box. If you prefe to not work a specific shift but do not have a commitment, please write prefer off. With proper communication and planning, we guarantee commitments; however, we cannot guarantee preferences. We will do our very best to honor your preferences, but the working relationship must be a two-way street.

	Thur	Fri	Sat	Sun	Mon	Tue	Wed
a.m.							
p.m.							

Requested number of shifts each week you would like to be scheduled:

Chapter 8:

Creating a Fair and Disciplined Environment

Several coworkers are mothers, fathers, and grandmothers while some are in high school, have dropped out of school, or are working on earning a degree. Some are part time, and others want as many hours as you are able to provide for them. Some people have been doing their job for years, and others are just getting started. Some are full of optimism, while others are full of fear and anxiety. Some people can't wait to arrive for work, and others can't wait to leave for the rest of their day.

The one thing all of your people have in common, however, is the fact that they are real people with real lives outside of the workplace. All have good days and all have-not-so-good days. All of your people, in reality, want and need the same things—security, acceptance, purpose, etc. The most effective leaders understand that all of their coworkers are real people with emotions. When we view our people as the role they are playing at work, we aren't able to connect with them through respect and empathy. Many managers want their coworkers to be fully engaged into the priorities of the company and to be enthusiastic about the goals of the management team. However, we often don't know what their goals are. How can we expect them to care about the desires of the company, if we as management do not understand what their goals are, and we only view them as the role they are playing at work?

The most critical role of management is in providing an environment of respect—respecting our coworkers, guests, and suppliers as the real people they are. Chick-fil-A sets the standard for creating an environment of respect. The key, is setting clearly defined expectations, and then leading those expectations as the role model. Accountability of rules has nothing to do with anger, conflict, or being a tyrant. It does, however, center on communication of what is expected and communication of when people do the right thing (praise) and the wrong thing (redirects). Again, anger and emotions have nothing to do with accountability. It is all about communication and follow-up.

Credibility for management is destroyed when coworkers are held to different standards. That is not to say there are no such things a gray areas. Gray areas are those situations where there is no *right* answer, depending on the perspective that something is being evaluated. Managing gray areas actually takes courage, since there will be people with different perspectives who frankly disagree with your position and are often vocal about their different perspectives. Gray areas will never go away. Effectively managing gray areas can be a bit easier when you seek the opinions of others. Truly asking and listening to the thoughts of others will help you in narrowing your decision to your best perspective as well as possibly learning for your own personal growth as a leader.

Accountability, on the other hand, is the one and only pathway to having a disciplined environment. And that accountability cannot be inconsistently applied to coworkers by allowing different standards for different coworkers. Many times, managers avoid accountability due to fear of losing a coworker or fear of the conflict that could arise from the accountability. An environment without fair and consistent accountability is a breeding ground for disengagement and higher coworker turnover. We often hold on to the problem coworkers while losing good coworkers due to their frustration. Those good coworkers leave in order to find new managers, not new jobs.

Let's look at one of the most egregious areas of management turning a blind eye—attendance. Attendance is really made of two challenges: tardiness and call-outs. First, let me say, both tardiness and call-outs are going to happen. Both, however, can be minimized when the fair and consistent accountability is applied.

Let's begin with tardiness. Tardiness can be minimized when management changes their behaviors and takes a personal approach to discipline for themselves.

If your goal is to create a fair but disciplined approach to tardiness, then here is a suggestion. Let's say your coworkers begin arriving at approximately 4:00 p.m. If you schedule your coworkers in at 4:00 p.m. with an understanding that preshift meetings begin at 4:05 p.m., then that five-minute *buffer* from their scheduled in time and the time you count as tardy allows for fairness. The key component is the manager's own self-discipline of starting preshift meetings at 4:05 p.m. That five-minute buffer allows the coworkers to arrive, look at positional charts and side-work charts, put their things away, etc. When the manager begins the 4:05 p.m. preshift meeting, they simply make note of any coworkers who are not in attendance. Afterward, the manager needs to take a disciplined approach of recording the tardy issue onto a tardy log, such as the one below.

Tardy Log

Store 202			Store Name: Gatlinburg, Tennessee
Name	Date	Scheduled In-Time	Reason for Tardiness
Jane Sladigin	9/1/2019	4:00	Traffic
Billy Overslept	9/2/2019	9:00	Did not hear alarm
Howie Smissin	9/2/2019	4:00	Thought he was scheduled in at 5:00

Keep in mind, there is no rule that states this tardy log must be typed; handwritten logs may be a better option. As a matter of fact, it is critical to keep all systems as simple and user-friendly as possible. Overcomplicating will simply lead to the discontinued use of the system, which means you are back to square one and not having a system in place at all. The easiest solution is to print several blank copies of the log each time you need more copies and then place onto a clipboard by the phone in the manager's office.

There also is no rule in establishing hard parameters such as three tardiness issues within ninety days results in a disciplinary measure. Creating such rules will more than likely motivate managers to once again turn a blind eye. I suggest 100 percent accuracy and adherence to the log. During orientations I explained there were no set rules referring to the number of infractions. I explained that we as management were 100 percent committed to recording all tardiness infractions. Once we saw a pattern of concern in someone's tardiness issues, as the general manager I would pull them aside and review the tardy log issues with them. I would then explain that I needed them to take care of these issues, or else we as a management team would continue to lose confidence that we could rely on them. I would then transfer our conversation onto a written form for documentation of the conversation with clear expectations. If the coworker's tardiness issues improve, great! If the issues continue, it is best to thank them for the work they have completed with you and then move forward with providing those hours to someone committed to being on time for their scheduled shifts.

Call-outs deserve their own tracking log, because in all reality, they are a different situation than tardiness. Call-outs are also part of life when it comes to any business with hurly coworkers. If call-outs are left undocumented, then the environment of the restaurant will be negatively impacted due to the increase of call-outs.

Call-out situations are also an opportunity for management to prove we are truly a *great place to work*. A typical response from an *average* manager when receiving a call-out phone call is similar to the following, "Well, I need for you to call around and get your shift covered." This style of leadership fails to take advantage of the opportunity in proving we are a great place to work. I would encourage a response similar to the following, "First, I am sorry to hear you are not feeling well. What time are you scheduled in today?"

My rule was simple with regards to call-outs. Call me as far in advance as you possibly can in order to give me a chance to do my job (managing the operations). If the coworker provided several hours of notice in regards to their call-out, then there was no problem, and I would be able to successfully fill that vacant position due to the strong relations I had with my team. If however, that coworker called me with less than two hours of notice, I would respond like this, "First, I am sorry you are not feeling well. As we discussed in orientation, I will take care of covering your shift. However, since this is less than two hours until your scheduled shift, we will need to review our policy once you are feeling better in order to improve our communication." A sample call-out log is shown below.

Call Out Log

Store 202				Store Name: Gatlinburg, Ten-
Name	Date	Scheduled In-Time	Time of Notification	Reason for Tardiness
Mary Lettucedown	9/3/2019	4:00 p.m.	3:45 p.m.	Stated she was sick
Nick Flewdacoop	9/3/2019	8:00 p.m.	NC/NC	Did not show for shift

Again, simplification in order to achieve a disciplined level of consistency from management using the call-out log is key to the success. A simple clipboard with handwritten notes is as easy as it gets and is a *no-excuse* approach to all managers utilizing 100 percent of the time with regards to coworker call-outs.

Chapter 9:

Coaching—Don't Just Walk on By

At the beginning of the 2019 college football season, Alabama head football coach Nick Saban had a record of 141 wins and 21 losses since becoming the head football coach in 2007. That is an amazing accomplishment, and even more amazing when you consider Alabama is a member of the toughest football conference in the National Collegiate Athletic Association (NCAA). Since 2011, Alabama has played for six of the eight national championships, winning four while never losing more than one regular-season game each year.

What is truly remarkable, however, is the number of head football coaches at other universities that once coached under Nick Saban as an assistant coach. The list includes Mark Dantonio (Michigan State University), Bobby Williams (formerly with Michigan State University), Jimbo Fisher (Texas A&M University), Will Muschamp (University of South Carolina), Derek Dooley (formerly with University of Tennessee), Jim McElwain (formerly with University of Florida), Lane Kiffin (Florida Atlantic University), Jeremy Pruitt (University of Tennessee), and Kirby Smart (University of Georgia). All of those universities that hired Nick Saban's assistant coaches were looking to replicate the success from Coach Saban's system.

So, I assume by now, some people reading this are wondering what coaching football has to do with coaching coworkers in my business, and my response is *everything*. Coaching people's behaviors is the same, regardless of whether it is on a football field or in a workplace setting. Would it be possible for Coach Saban to reach his level of success if he simply walked on by when he witnessed his players performing incorrectly? Absolutely not!

Coaching in the simplest form is the positive acknowledgement of behaviors that are correct and the redirection of behaviors that are incorrect. It's really that simple. The most common roadblock of effective coaching is the lack of knowledge by the coach. Think about it—you cannot coach what you do not know. If a recipe is made incorrectly, and you as the leader do not truly know the recipe, then it is very likely you will avoid the situation by pretending not to see the questionable behavior. If on the other hand, you have skill mastery of a behavior (recipe, in this example), then it should be almost impossible for you to not coach (redirect) the wrong behavior.

So, again, there are two forms of coaching feedback that I will focus on—praise and redirects. Praise is the verbal, public acknowledgement of a behavior when it is the correct behavior. If we continue with the recipe example, it is critical to praise the behaviors of the cook when they make the pepperoni pizza perfectly according to the recipe. That confirmation is inspiring to the coworker, and thus they are likely to continue the correct behavior due to the re-enforcement of the correct behavior.

Redirects are the verbal, nonpublic correction of a behavior that is being executed incorrectly. Again, with the example of a recipe such as pepperoni pizza, if the cook is incorrectly making the pepperoni pizza, then a strong leader will say, "Time-out, let's look at the recipe for this pizza." By stopping and addressing the incorrect behavior, you are sending a message that recipes are non-negotiable. Again, keep in mind, you cannot coach what you do not know. So if you as a leader do not know the basics of your business, you are likely to avoid those conversations in order to ensure your lack of knowledge is not exposed.

Teams that execute at a high level do so because of leadership that ensures a high level of execution through shoulder-to-shoulder coaching and teaching. Balanced leaders look for opportunities to praise every bit as much as they look for opportunities to redirect behaviors. High levels of execution are not the result of good luck. High levels of execution are the results of setting clear expectations followed by effective coaching (praise and redirects) and not by simply being lucky.

By striving to find opportunities to praise and redirect behaviors, a balanced leader will try to be fifty-fifty with their praises and redirects. When we praise too much with no redirects, we are seen as weak leaders who are only interested in how people feel about them. When we redirect too much with no praise, we are seen as leaders who are negative and never pleased. Balanced leadership means we are skilled in both praise and redirect opportunities, and we look for opportunities throughout the day for both types of coaching.

Below is a simple form that should be used to capture the most impactful praise of the day and the most impactful redirect of the day. This is a great practice for assistant managers in order to help develop that skill area with their leadership. By documenting the most impactful praise and redirect of the day, the general manager can assess the leadership-skill level of the assistant manager and actually coach that assistant manager.

Employee Coaching Card

Employee name _____

Manager name _____Date _____

Details of praised/redirected behavior: (circle one)

_____
_____
_____

The completed forms are a great tool for discussions during the weekly manager's meeting. By quickly sharing the information with one another during the manager's meeting, all managers are then dialed into the coaching moments throughout the week. This shared information strengthens the management team and helps move the managers from a manager group to a management team.

Chapter 10:

Internal Communication

General Robert E. Lee surrendered his troops to General Ulysses S. Grant at Appomattox Court House, Virginia, on April 9, 1865, ending the four-year American Civil War. Why then was the last significant Civil War battle fought in Texas on May 13, 1865? For starters, there was no such thing as CNN, Fox News, Twitter, Snapchat, texting, iPhones, or phones of any kind since Alexander Graham Bell didn't receive the US patent for the telephone until 1876. News in the 1800s traveled by mouth. In today's world we have all of the luxuries of modern-day miracles for communication, yet we still struggle with communication. I would even go as far as saying *poor communication is the root of most problems we face in our businesses.*

So why do we struggle with communication? From my experience, we often struggle with communication for one simple reason—we don't plan. Without a plan, we fail in our preparation to communicate with our people. Communication in the simplest form consists of the following three factors: planning, setting expectations, and follow-up.

Planning. The number one job of any leader is to bring a management group together as a management team. A management group is two or more individuals, all on different pages with different focuses or priorities. There is no cohesion and no game plan for improvement. Each person is focused on their own messaging to the team, which often leads to frustration with coworkers due to the varied guidance between managers. A management team on the other hand is two or more individuals who are together with their priorities and messaging to the team. A management team has a plan for attacking the operation's most significant challenges. A management team communicates the same message to the coworkers due to the shared belief in the plan for that particular week.

The basis for moving a management group to a management team is the commitment of having a weekly manager meeting. The goal of the weekly meeting is to identify the top operational challenges for the next seven days. I can remember scheduling a weekly manager meeting when I was assigned to a new operation. I was often amazed that the managers I was now working with would arrive at the first meeting with their lunch in hand, yet nothing to write with or take notes on. My first task was to reset their thinking in regards to our weekly manager meeting. I explained they were welcome to eat their lunch when they thought it was best; however, during the forty minutes to one hour opportunity we had for our meeting, there was no time for eating lunch. This was our business meeting for planning our week. This was our one and only opportunity to begin the new week with a unified focus on our top priorities. Most importantly, I expected full engagement into the conversations and therefore had to change their mindset of a meeting, in which they expected, and I would be entertaining them.

I assigned a challenge for each manager at the initial meeting. That challenge was for them to come each week to our business meeting prepared to lead discussions on their department, identifying the biggest challenge for their department. As a group I wanted all of us to have input on how we would be able to work with our coworkers that week in solving those challenges. To me, this was very simple concept: How do we make certain that, this time next week, we are better than we are today? This is growth, and growth is necessary for any business to survive. Remember Kodak, Nokia, Xerox, Blockbuster, IBM, Blackberry, Myspace, Polaroid, Motorola, Circuit City, and Toys "R" Us? All were major players at one time; however, without change and improvement, your business can fade away.

Setting expectations. Each department head should come to the weekly business meeting having looked at their department and identified their biggest challenges. All leaders at the meeting should engage into conversations on how the management team as a whole will aid the department head in improving that challenge. The plan for attacking that challenge should be captured during the discussions of the weekly business meeting in writing, in order to be shared with the coworkers.

All week, management should hold preshift meetings with the coworkers addressing the challenges identified during the weekly business meeting. These preshift meetings should be short, to-the-point conversations centered on the three to four topics identified during the business meeting. The repetition of the preshift meeting communication helps to set the expectations as well as provide clarity on the *whys*. When coworkers understand the rationale behind decisions, they are much more likely to buy-in to the solutions. Without the plan, however, these preshift meetings often do not happen.

Follow-up. The third factor referenced in effective communication is the follow-up or coaching, which occurs after having set the expectations. Again, as discussed in chapter nine, coaching in the simplest form is identifying observed behaviors through either a moment of *praise* or a moment of *redirecting* coworker behaviors. When a *management group* (all managers working on their own agenda) tries to attack a change that is needed, you often find only one manager communicating about that behavior. When a *management team* (all managers aligned and working on the same challenges) attacks a problem, there is strength in numbers. That aligned leadership shows unity in the *management team*, which has a similar positive impact of having both mom and dad aligned with their children. Division creates confusion and frustration, whereas alignment creates a sense of strength and focus. When coworkers hear the similar praising or redirecting of behaviors from all of the managers, there is power in the leadership. Coworkers actually enjoy working in a structured environment with consistency from management. This is exactly what was referenced earlier when discussing coworkers leaving to find new managers.

Finally, it is important to note the difference between anger and passion when discussing redirect-coaching moments. Again, it is critical to always redirect behaviors in private; none of us want to be embarrassed among our peers. Effective leaders are able to eliminate anger from the communication style while still being passionate about the coworker, guest, and shareholder experience. Anger is actually a sign of weakness; however, unfortunately some people mistakenly confuse anger with passion. Nonetheless, an environment of true respect is not possible if leaders are unable to control their anger when addressing behaviors with coworkers.

Chapter 11:

Developing Your Managers for the Future

I often wonder what causes some people to be reluctant to teach their associate managers all that they can teach them. Is it fear? Do they fear that someone will actually grow to be better than they are? Do they fear that they will lose their right-hand manager to a promotion or to another opportunity? Do they fear that someone might teach them a better way to complete certain tasks? Are all of these fears, in addition to other fears not even mentioned, a reality in their mind? What else could it be, if it is not fear? Why would someone want to withhold information that would help others grow in their development? Fear and/or selfishness—I am unable to see it any other way.

On the other hand, what causes some people to want to fully develop all of their associate managers? What motivates some leaders to want others to grow as much as possible? Is it that they are secure in their own mind and truly want the best for others? Is it that they enjoy helping others reach their goals, even if it means they lose that person to another opportunity or location? Do some people simply want what is best for others without worry of the impact on their business? Are some people simply so secure in their ability to teach that they feel they are able to develop and give up great talent with more talent coming right behind?

I guess the answer to these questions boil down to fear, selfishness, empathy, and the impact of a challenge. Some are natural-born developers, and some are natural-born hoarders. My belief is this: if you are a selfish person who does not want the best situation for others, you are going to lose that person one way or another at some point. Eventually, they will quit on you.

There are major benefits of developing others. During the time that you are able to have high-level leaders as part of your management team, in theory, your operation should execute on a very high and consistent level. With proper development of your associate managers, management turnover will be lower as associate managers believe someone really cares about their future. When you as a leader care about someone's future and development, you are also caring for that person's family, and they will not leave you for another company. On the other hand, when people feel they work for a selfish leader, who only cares about their own personal needs and goals, then eventually a time will come when the associate manager feels it is in their best interest to move on. Other benefits to developing your associate managers is the improved quality of life for everyone on the management team. By having a highly developed management team, there are fewer weak links in the chain, thus improved operations and ultimately increased profit.

One other possibility not mentioned as why some leaders may not develop others for the future is that maybe they simply do not know the tactical approach for teaching others through a systematic way. Most companies have a solid manager in training (MIT) course. But once a manager completes the MIT program, many companies fail to have a structured pathway for associate managers to continue their growth. Below is a format for addressing a structured learning system of management development, with a few thoughts I think are critical to understand:

1. The GM is responsible for scheduling the biweekly management one-on-one development meeting on the manager's schedule for everyone to see. Rule number one for GMs is to never blow off a scheduled management development one-on-one.
2. The GM is responsible for showing up for the scheduled management development one-on-one meeting. There may be times where it is necessary to reschedule the one-on-one; however, never just let it go.
3. The GM should not be leading the conversation; the associate manager should be leading the discussion. The GM is a resource of knowledge; however, the associate manager is the one who really knows what makes sense to them and what does not. GMs cannot read minds, so let the associate manager lead the discussions.

Tips on how to prepare for developmental one-on-ones are listed below:
1. Schedule the one-on-ones; place onto the manager's schedule. Schedule the one-on-ones on a regular basis, at least monthly. Newer managers will benefit from more scheduled one-on-ones, possibly weekly or biweekly. Never cancel the one-on-one. If it must be rescheduled, then reschedule. However, make certain to always follow thru with the scheduled one-on-ones.
2. Have the right mindset: do not overthink the meeting. The conversation should be informal and free. Try to find a place where the fewest interruptions will occur. Although some prep work can be beneficial, the direct report should understand they are in the driver's seat and should set the direction of the meeting. The direct report should do the most talking.
3. Be an active listener. Listening is one of the most important skills effective leaders have. It is impossible for us to learn when we are talking. Allowing our minds to be distracted can prevent the one-on-one from being effective. It is critical to actively listen in order to understand the depth of development needed by your team. By having strong listening skills, you are more likely to build a stronger relationship with your team. Most importantly, take notes and repeat their points in order to show connection.
4. Be open minded. While running these one-on-ones, it is important for leaders to set the example by showing they are open to feedback about themselves and their business. Remember, there are multiple ways to get to the end point. Be open-minded to feedback of personal change for yourself. This is a sign of strength not weakness. A strong leader is more focused on driving results, not ego.
5. How to wrap-up the one-on-ones: make sure to wrap up the critical talking points and discuss the action plan to be carried out between now and the next scheduled one-on-one. Review and agree on the most critical actions for development.

When one-on-ones are conducted properly, your team will feel engaged and valued. Encourage the direct report by looking for the action items between today's one-on-one and the next scheduled one-on-one. Praise and redirects also apply for your managers.

Management Development: One-on-One Questions

1. General check-in questions:
2. Tell me about your week.
3. What's on your mind this week?
4. Last time we spoke, you said _____ was a challenge for you, how is that going?
5. What are your plans and priorities this week?
6. Alignment questions: (This is where you want to see how connected or aligned an individual feels to the organization.)
7. How confident do you feel with where the company is going?
8. Do you have any questions about the recent change of _____?
9. What do you feel the company priorities should be?
10. Progress questions: (It is important to understand how people feel they are progressing and if they feel they are experiencing growth.)
11. What has challenged you this past quarter?
12. What has gone well/not so well in the last ninety days?
13. What is the one most important thing you have learned this period?
14. Do you feel confident in how your department is progressing? Why or why not?
15. How are you and your team progressing toward your established goals?
16. How are things going with your people? Who are your biggest challenges?
17. What feedback do you have for me in ways I can support you?
18. Career aspirations: (Career aspirations and goals are important in order to keep people engaged.)
19. When you think of yourself in two years, what comes to mind?
20. What are two or three new skills you would like to learn at work?
21. How are you progressing toward your bigger career and life goals?
22. Is there someone in the district you would like to learn from?
23. What progress have you made this month on your career goals?

24. Questions to close the one-on-one: (Ending your one-on-one with actionable questions keeps the loop open for feedback.)
25. What commitments do you have between today and next month?
26. What can I help you with between now and next month?
27. Is there anything we didn't cover that you would like to discuss?

Chapter 12:

Leadership: What Exactly Does That Look Like?

As a newly promoted district manager years ago, I was on a flight in order to attend a meeting at our corporate office. As I was flying down for the meeting, I began to think about the six general managers I worked with in my district. In all reality, I had three general managers who were very effective leaders, and yet I also had three general managers who were very ineffective. As I thought about these leaders, I began to think about the characteristics shared by the three successful leaders. I made a list of those characteristics on a notepad that I still have today and are listed below:

- Team respect. They earned the respect of their teams, because they are fair and consistent. They lead by example.
- Integrity. They base their choices on doing what is right, and they expect the same from the people on their team. It is not okay to lie, cheat, or steal in their environment.
- Optimistic. They have a true belief that they control their destiny. They don't believe that success is the result of luck. They believe they drive their own path to success.
- Accountability. They provide honest feedback to their people. They praise when people do the right thing, and they redirect when people don't do the right thing. No one on the team is above the rules and

expectations.
- Know their people. They see their people as the mothers and fathers that they are. They understand a college student's pressure outside of the work environment. They know and understand the goals of all of their people.
- Unselfish. They truly want others to succeed. They are not afraid to teach and develop others in order for others to reach their goals.
- Disciplined. They themselves are disciplined in their approach to business through systems. They teach others the value of a disciplined approach to life.
- Motivators. They understand how to inspire people to be their best. They enjoy being competitive, because they have a desire to be the best and are willing to do the things others are not willing to do in order to reach that success.
- Planning and organizing. They have systems in place and back-up plans just in case. They create schedules based on what is best for the business, not what is simply best for themselves.
- Follow processes and systems. They have systems in place for all aspects of their operations. They teach those systems to their teams and expect nothing less than 100 percent commitment to the systems.

What I found to be interesting is that of the ten shared characteristics of my successful general managers, only two characteristics (planning and organizing, and follow processes and systems) are so-called *technical* skills. The remaining eight shared characteristics could be argued as *people* skills. If that is true, then 80 percent of what drives effective leadership could be people skills, while only 20 percent are considered technical skills.

So, what does real leadership look like in action? How do you even define leadership? If you Google the word "leadership," you will find the following: "the action of leading a group of people or an organization." You will see words such as guidance, direction, authority, control, management, etc. I believe leadership (action taken) is defined by the situation that leader is currently dealing with. The situation is going to dictate what actions an effective leader is going to take. In other words, there is no one *style* of leadership that can be used for all situations. In our personal lives, we do not treat a toilet overflowing onto the floor in the same manner as we would react to adjusting the thermostat for our air conditioning. We would have a different sense of urgency in those two situations. Thus one *style* of leadership simply does not fit all situations. Let's look at some different styles of leadership and what they might look like.

The Dominant Style. This is a style of leadership where someone must step up and take control. There is no asking people about their opinion and no flexibility in what you are asking people to do. It is a *do as I ask, and do it now* type of leadership. The dominant style of leadership is best used in emergency situations or in a situation where operations must have a turnaround in performance. In these emergency/performance-turnaround situations, someone has to step up and give definite direction. If the building is on fire, you are not going to ask, "What does everyone think we should do?" On the other hand, just because you use the dominant style of leadership in certain situations, that doesn't mean you have to be rude or abrasive. It simply means you have to be decisive, clear, and direct in your guidance. If the dominant style is overused, then your people will not think for themselves, and their development may stop because they will rely on you for making all decisions. When the dominant style is used in the proper scenarios, then it is a very effective style, which every leader should be able to use.

The Keep-Up-with-Me Style. This is a style of leadership where you roll up your sleeves and lead by example. With the keep-up-with-me style, you are creating credibility with your team by showing what is possible. It is almost a challenge that you are placing right in front of them. There are many positives associated with this keep-up-with-me style. However if overused, many leaders do not see the larger picture of what is happening in their business.

One of those previously mentioned general managers who struggled with leadership skills overused the keep-up-with-me style. During peak periods he would run throughout the restaurant often bussing tables. When I asked him why he didn't put more servers on the schedule, he replied, "Because if I add more servers, they will not make as much money, and they will quit." There are many arguments against his rationale; however, for this discussion, the point that I tried helping him understand is about everything that he is missing by being the busser for his servers. His restaurant was in a mall, and that mall provided many mall coworkers who wanted to eat their lunch with us. However, since he chose to run with fewer servers, his hosts would often run a false wait, even though there were tables available. The mall coworkers were on very short breaks, and therefore many of them chose to go to the food court due to the false wait. The general manager was so busy bussing tables, he could not see the potential guests who wanted to spend their money with him leaving for the food court! You cannot overuse the keep-up-with-me style. Step into the situation in order to coach and show how to execute, but get back out quickly in order to see the larger picture.

The What-Do-You-Think Style. CEOs have board members, and presidents have cabinet advisors. Critical thinkers want to gather as much data as possible before making important decisions. There are no rules that state leaders have to have all of the answers. As a matter of fact, the best leaders are confident enough to seek other people's opinions. The downside, however, to the what-do-you-think style of leadership is time. Time can be wasted if debates arise, and the leader lacks the skill in getting the conversation back onto the track of being productive. There is a very fine balance of seeking other's opinions in order to create healthy, productive discussions and knowing when it is time to move back to the dominant style when you sense a stall in productivity. The final benefit I will mention in regards to the what-do-you-think style of leadership is the amount of buy-in you create by asking others for their opinions. Research has shown an increase in engagement when a person's input was part of the solution to a problem. Utilizing this style during manager meetings can be a very effective time for discussions. Again I caution to be aware of time and know when it is time to move to a different style!

The I-See-You Style of Leadership. One of the most critical skills for leaders is the ability to see what is and is not happening right around them. In order to have this operational vision, you first have to know what you are talking about. Let's take recipes for example. If a leader in the restaurant industry does not know the recipes of their restaurant's food, then they will not be able to see or know when things are right or wrong. You can't coach what you don't know! If on the other hand, the leader has skill mastery in recipe knowledge, then he or she will be able to know when things are right or wrong. The follow-up of coaching that coworker once you have the vision is the most critical part of the I-see-you style of leadership. In other words, effective leaders will *praise* coworkers who are executing correctly and will *redirect* coworker behaviors when they see things that are incorrect. If you do not provide this feedback, I challenge whether you are truly acting as a leader. A good rule-of-thumb is to strive to be fifty-fifty with your *praise* and with your *redirects*. No one wants to work with that leader who is constantly focused on what's wrong—constantly focused on the negatives. On the other hand, if all you do as a leader is praise, then eventually coworkers will tune you out. Your credibility in their eyes will be weak because of all of the constant praising and lack of ability to redirect opportunities. The best leaders are balanced in their praise and redirects.

The Roadmap Style. The roadmap style of leadership is the style used when a vision or path needs to result in change or improvement. It is the *here's-where-we-are-headed* style and *here's how we will get there*. This style sets the stage for changes in the future by addressing the tactics of how the goal or changes can be achieved. There is a balance of the dominant style of leadership and the what-do-you-think style, which, when used properly, is typically very motivating and inspiring.

The most common downside of the roadmap style of leadership is if the vision is wrong or if there is a lack of follow-thru. Credibility is damaged when the roadmap style is used excessively and/or without completion. Great leaders know when things are going off course and changes are needed. The roadmap style of leadership is used for correcting the course of operations by painting a clear picture of where the operation is headed and exactly how we will get there. Remember, great leaders don't stay wrong for long.

The Parental Style. This style of leadership provides security by striving to create a family environment within the team. The parental style builds security by creating an environment where people are treated as the real people they are rather than treating people based on their role in your business. This is a style that focuses on true respect. That respect is expected to and from everyone within your team.

The parental style of leadership is a very positive style, unless favoritism or inconsistency of expectations becomes an issue. Clear guidelines and adherence are an important factor with this style. When guidelines are clear and coworkers are fairly held accountable, the environment is a very positive, secure environment. Holding yourself accountable and being the example of treating people with respect is the key to building this environment.

Leadership Balance. The best leaders understand and utilize all of the different styles of leadership depending upon the situation. When mastery of all of the styles is accomplished and practiced, the leader instinctively knows which style will be best served in that moment. Since all of the styles of leadership have their benefits and drawbacks, no one style is *better* than the others. It is impossible to use only one style of leadership and say, "this is my style." Constantly flowing from one style of leadership to another is the mark of a good leader. Knowing which style is best for the situation is the mark of a great leader.

Chapter 13:

Closing: The Law of Business

There really are no shortcuts in life. Survival of the fittest not only plays out in nature, but it also determines business success in industries that must rely upon people as coworkers. With record unemployment, coworkers have choices, and their choices are based on their needs. In addition to competitive pay, coworkers are looking for security. Security in the workplace comes from many different aspects. Some are looking for personal career development in order to grow and gain more responsibility, while others are simply looking for a fair and consistent environment of respect.

The systems discussed throughout this book are not difficult to understand, yet why do so many leaders fail to implement these practices? Why do so many businesses constantly turn coworkers when other businesses in the same industry and same market have healthy coworker retention? There are many answers to that question; however, the three answers that I believe whole-heartedly are as follows:

1. Coworker turnover is a choice. It is not luck, bad or good, that impacts the decisions of selection, onboarding and training, and workplace environment. All three of those outcomes are determined by choice—choices ultimately set by the leadership of that particular business.
2. Coworker turnover results are not *soft* skills but rather *money* skills. If a business has a money-handling issue, food-cost issue, or unproductive labor issue, leadership often quickly determines a plan for improving

those results. There is a sense of urgency to get to the root cause in order to correct the issue. However, when it comes to the tremendous waste of money accounting for the high-turnover environment, there seems to often be a lack of sense of urgency in getting to the root problem. This is possibly due to the root problem actually being the behaviors and decisions of the leadership. As a leader, you must own the money skills of coworker turnover.

3. Coworker turnover is not determined by the market. Every market in the world will have businesses that have extremely high-coworker turnover, and every market will have businesses with extremely low-coworker turnover. Although some markets may present more challenges than others, that simply means the length of time it takes to reach the healthy retention levels may take longer. If a strong leader is placed in the *tough* hiring market, ultimately the strong leader will surround themselves with the right core of people, and turnover results will become healthy. If a poor leader is placed in a market that is typically easier to find good, qualified people, then eventually that poor leader will still reach high levels of coworker turnover. The market only determines the length of time to reach the level of healthy retention.

The 1 + 2 = 3 philosophy is completely about order—the order in which a leadership team must abide in building their business. It is unrealistic to expect to maximize profit just because of a goal that exists in your mind. Profit is ultimately impossible without guests or clients. It is also unrealistic to expect to provide exceptional products and services to your guests or clients simply due to a goal you have in your mind. It takes real people, fully engaged and trained in position in order to build guest results that will build your business. It is unrealistic to think you can build a business with poor customer results from underdeveloped, unengaged coworkers.

The entire message from this book is that business results begin with the leadership team and staff of that business. The good news is that, as a leader, you really do have total control of the selection, onboarding and training, and workplace environment of your business, which is exactly what drives your people results.

1 + 2 = 3

As you move through your journey of leading your business, I would wish you luck; however, I promise, luck will have nothing to do with it! The choices you make determine your outcome.

Author Biography

Christopher T. Henderson graduated from Virginia Tech with a BS degree in hospitality and tourism management and later served on the board of directors for Virginia Tech's Hospitality and Tourism Management program. During his years at Virginia Tech, he completed an internship with Marriott International as part of his degree requirements. Upon graduation from Virginia Tech, Christopher was one of only six graduating seniors chosen for Hyatt Hotels Corporation's Corporate Management Trainee program. He began his career as a management trainee at the Park Hyatt Washington, DC. After completion of the management training program with Hyatt Hotels Corporation, he began his career in human resources as an employment manager and benefits manager at both the Park Hyatt Washington, DC and Hyatt Regency Washington on Capitol Hill.

After relocating to Orlando, Florida, Christopher began his restaurant career at ground level. Christopher went on to hold multiunit-level positions with three national brands as well as two privately owned restaurant companies. Throughout his career, he was awarded *GM of the Year* and three-time *District Manager of the Year* and was the recipient of the *Chairman and President's Award*—the highest honor awarded. As a general manager, his restaurant was chosen from more than four hundred corporate-owned restaurants by the founder and CEO to train the first-ever, franchise-management team in the history of the company. The founder and CEO stated in a letter, "This is what we want our franchise restaurants to look and feel like," which was framed and displayed upon the wall of the operation. Later in his career, his span of responsibility included a region of fifty-three restaurant operations as well as nine district managers. Throughout his career, Christopher was tasked with the responsibility of leading thirty-one new restaurant openings.

Christopher's philosophy has always been grounded in the human resource lessons learned in the classrooms at Virginia Tech as well as his early career exposure with both Marriott International and Hyatt Hotels Corporation. He has effectively applied the lessons throughout this book at each company he worked and was able to consistently achieve the top-level results of the company with these systems. His 1 + 2 = 3 philosophy continues as the *true north* in driving long-term, sustained, positive same-store guest traffic, sales, and profits. Christopher's step-by-step approach of building great teams, as the most basic building block of leadership, creates a foundation in which true success and growth is not only possible but probable.